Three Chapbooks

Three Poets

# Three Chapbooks
# Three Poets

Rodger Moody
Carol Durak
John P Harn

THREE CHAPBOOKS / THREE POETS
© Rodger Moody, Carol Durak, and John P Harn, respectively.

First Flowstone Press edition • March 2024
ISBN-13: 978-1-945824-64-7

Cover art by Siena Sanderson, *Harmonia*, 2000, 9"x12",
ink drawing over gesso on wood
Cover photo by Megan Beck
Cover design by Ryan Forsythe and John Harn

Interior design by Ryan Forsythe
Photo of Rodger Moody by Dashiell Moody
Photo of Carol Durak by Manuel One Sparrow
Photo of John Harn by Aya Harn

Flowstone Press,
an Imprint of Left Fork
www.leftforkbooks.com

This project is dedicated to the memory of
Ralph J. Salisbury (1926-2017)

A celebrated professor, mentor, poet, and storyteller noted for kindness, Ralph left an indelible impression on thousands of early-career writers and dedicated his work, as he once said, "to the tribe of the world."

*Though I have lived and worked among the intelligentsia of many nations, my writing comes from being a questing, mixed-race, working-class individual... My work is offered to the spirit of human goodness, which unites all people...*

- Ralph Salisbury -

Contents

Self-Portrait / Sixteen Sevenlings    1
   by Rodger Moody

Hymn Postponement    23
   by Carol Durak

Something from Nothing    51
   by John Peter Harn

Self-Portrait / Sixteen Sevenlings

Rodger Moody

Sevenling (He longed for)


He longed for three things about farm
life: the morning rooster, good compost
in the garden, corn cobs glowing in the fireplace.

He had no use for strangers
selling Bibles, children who refused
to weed the garden, well-meaning neighbors.

The countryside belongs to the swallows.

Sevenling  (He lived for)


He lived for three things:
work gloves, sun in the morning,
the deep blue Midwest sky.

He didn't care for outsiders,
stiff prairie winds, a woman's
cold coffee. He practiced

how to talk while plowing flat fields.

Sevenling (He read magazines)


He read magazines in back of study hall,
daydreamed of piloting jetliners to far off destinations,
longed to kiss the only lawyer in town's daughter.

A buddy parked a white Pontiac convertible
with a cracked block in his driveway — the Chesterfields were his idea,
the open road another thing altogether. Someone has

the missing pages of the family dictionary.

Sevenling (The rub is)


The rub is to see where you are
looking, not lifting the veil,
or plucking invisible strings

that connect everything. He disliked the
easily led, the two-faced middleman,
the first hint of liver spots. Everything,

he said, turns to shit.

Sevenling (Three things he loved)


Three things he loved about Pi Day:
stories about parties in other countries,
word games with numbers as answers,

pie. He hated to learn of the mind's infinite
potential, mayhem as natural as water, endless
memorization with no pie to eat.

Math and barking ravens all around us.

Sevenling (What of all the dreary)


What of all the dreary years slogging
the warehouse floor, the patchy plywood, the com-
puter and the withholding technician.

The tender girl who stocks the reach-in
cooler, her songs and libidinous dance
when we are alone, the existential disconnect.

Chet Baker on the radio softly following a sad song.

Sevenling (A welder, toothless)


A welder, toothless men wearing goggles
work hand-held grinders beside his tired shack,
the night darkening like the line foreman.

Outside, the Milky Way full of twinkling
energy, his father's brother wants to know
if anyone bothers him, the company showers cold, dirty.

He drives the back road home with the radio off.

Sevenling (Dad loved just)

Dad loved just three things:
bowling, long hours at the steel mill,
how the windshield wipers of his old truck

shook. He had no use for neighbors,
vacations, or the nuances
of political talk. No one ever saw him

with a chocolate bar.

Sevenling (A boy had)


A boy had three dreams:
snow, his own room,
a father he could talk to.

But there was only the long walk
to school, cold cereal every morning,
a mother who lived in the past.

No one will love you, she said.

Sevenling (The cinder block warehouse)

The cinder block warehouse dark,
a semi idles hard down the rutted
alleyway, the walk-in freezer ceiling

drips. The sliding door is off its track,
a muffin has been left too long in the toaster
oven, and the boss is forgetful.

He slips back under the water now.

Sevenling (As a boy he wanted)


As a boy he wanted just three things:
a lower basketball hoop, long underwear,
to see Lake Michigan.

He roamed the erosion gullies of the gravel
pit behind his grandparent's farm, hated water,
and his grandfather's gruff voice.

Somehow he was never tall enough.

Sevenling (The cul-de-sac is)


The cul-de-sac is on a hill,
our house is a duplex, north of town,
the Coburg Hills shrouded in fog.

The high ceiling of the living room,
the balcony of the loft, bring to mind
tall trees delirious in sun and wind.

The quiet street is almost sad.

Sevenling (He wished for)


He wished for three signs:
the green light, a dog
chasing its tail, photos of nudes.

He disliked coy girls,
wet hair in the workplace,
a woman with a point of view.

He couldn't understand the unmade bed.

Sevenling (He shrugged off)


He shrugged off three things about
boot camp: the small lies, the big lies,
subtle psychological manipulation.

He hated stories others told
about girls back home, marching,
orders for breakfast, lunch, dinner.

Thoughts belong to no one.

Sevenling (The dirty warehouse)


The dirty warehouse is cold
this morning. He's wet from the rainy
bike ride against traffic. He wants breakfast.

Shrink-wrapped pallets hug the wall
against the alleyway. He hates counting
returns. The hand truck's unfailing

flat tire. He remembers the job wasn't to last.

Sevenling (He parked in his easy)


He parked in his easy chair for the evening
after work. The gritty steel mill and cigars
he only chewed languished on the other side

of the river. Morning the street dark he drove
the narrow back road toward smokestacks. He
ogled the silent blue sky, swilled coffee.

His tired pickup held the winding road.

Acknowledgments

the *Kerf*: "Sevenling (He longed for)"

*The Oregonian*: "Sevenling (He lived for)"

*Self-Portrait / Sixteen Sevenlings* by Rodger Moody was the winner of Bright Hill Press's Poetry Chapbook Competition, originally published in 2013.

# Hymn Postponement

Carol Durak

"Each time, when the record ended, he said something like: 'Hear that, man. Hear that.'"

Hayden Carruth

Instructions from the Children

Take the back stairs to the front porch.
Set the table as if we have eaten.
When we were born,
the baskets meant for us to sleep in
had just finished unraveling.

From the dyed reeds, a puddle of limp.
When something functions well,
for example, wind, as it sails beyond
the beds of reeds, give opposition
credit. Give gravity flexibility:

going upstairs includes:
run through tall grass. Each step
is a story. Each story, the next step—
There's a nervousness upstairs
like it doesn't want any walls.

Familial

Children keep on: bearded sons, daughters with white hair—
I'm one, and because of it my pulse bears
clues: they run through me, and yet, I ran original—I was
mean but worth rescue. There was a blur—
In our mother's gaze, I read, "Let things go."


From her room, there was a stir—Mother's wandered off.
Our mother (daughter and sister, too) has wandered off and left us.
Will her changing shape unglue us? We have our shifting
sibling memories, our one collective view: it runs through us:
across the distant moors, our blue heather slice of it.

I Will Wait for Eternity


but in the meantime, though my bark-colored hair
is disheveled as torn up roots and brush
tangled in slow parts of the Huron,
I have taken to heart a couple questions.

The mind, as it flows like the current—you see,
I've paired this going with your name
the way I pair with infinity
the slow ripples in a mallard's wake.

The divine that swirls around, that swims
through debris and rubble, through the branches
and strange rags caught along the banks
of the Huron—how in the world to spell it out?

Even if I could, would the river take it down
as if I had tied my words to a millstone?

Sparse Place

The indefinite horizon lured me.
Sun's low, but there's no sign of it,
or it's been removed. Nothing is
blue here or green or embellished like lace.
Snapped short, the trees' branches, those
that remain, are three-quarters up.
Tall dark trunks, some angled as if plunged
like poles into sand, are a stark commune
of bleak. Someone's vision of hell,
not mine. I translate: beckoning grove.
It looks through death. No electrical wires
in sight. I've heard of Pine Barrens.
Chances are this place is nameless.
No time-sensitive invite on my part.
No glare. My eyes are fine here, getting
better—there's the line, edge of knife
sharp, it separates the stone-white sky
from the bone-grey land. Edge of
knife thin, it tells me, having seen it,
this place is my escort from *here I am*
to *where are you* until we converge.

II

This Crossroad

means business, not for lazy-eyed visits.
Like beanpole-loneliness stark
against the sky, maybe a crucified groan or a pothole
disposition dragged you out.

Don't get fooled. These daemonesque squalls,
these deep-sunk throbs are twisters.
They're false-hooded bliss, a careless tryst
gone wrong. Don't get fooled:

it's them again: those daemonesque squalls.
Don't get fooled. They've no place else to go.
They're commissioned. You might see pearls.
I saw my pulse pulse-out into the ether.

I should have backed off, spun around
before the prophet-like crow dipped low,
or the crow-like prophet on steroids tripped aglow,
and dropped my name at the crossroad.

Voice

You were in the nectar.
The flower was in her throat.

Savage and fearless, song hung
in the distant bramble. You see,

torn hearts in the harrow and her thoughts
grew tinged.

You were in the hidden.
The hidden within her sung

like the mourning songs of Greek women,
the truths of Tim Buckley, soaring, searching—

In the jazz club she clung
to divine company drinking

deeply. Nina Marie's lone voice
trailed off—
        *like a hummin'bird*

*hummin' hummin'*
        *hummin' hummin'*

*hummin'bird—*

Familiar Stranger

Not like a preacher's rant,
but the man on the corner's got
fire, a standing appointment
with dawn, and an alchemy of
curses with enough flow
that sleepers in tall buildings
absorb his voice into the last
slips of their dreams. As fast
as a wasp gets mad a quick jeer
stabs me on the second floor.
"On schedule," I whisper. There is
no heaven, no hell, just rooms,
sidewalks, and traffic that will soon
drown out his throat-exotics.
Like a gambler will he kiss
Dawn? Will she deal a golden
flush? I doubt that she'll run
through the streets lifting her veils
like a goddess. My relationship
with wreckage is as private as why,
having just crossed Catherine
and heading up Division, he
takes off his shoes and rhymes
barefoot as if on nails.

Hymn Postponement

It's the bottom worst half
of the day because hurt comes up
into my window and swerves an odd pitch
through my evening norms.

I know this plaint: its cry

presses higher, moves this line

into this one. I know it like a headache,

it's anti-chaconne, and I know

if ignored, it will chop and stall, drag down

neat, stammer, howl—and reek dread if

I close the window

and settle into the chair of my poem's
last line, if I write: *Let the vespertine
songbird pipe up*, or *When will the
vespertine songbird pipe up…*

Pulse Note

Get ready, old heart, go ahead and detrain
that train of thought. Descend from its platform.

You wanted reprieve, and
                          now, in accommodating night, listen:
another train's coming—switching tracks.

//

Space to Proceed

What is more diligent than dust,
more rock-breaking than the saxifrage flower,
more built-to-last than a sapling
beat down by a thunderstorm;
and which would be more
preferable: to turn your blunder
into a comedy or to be carried off stage
as if planned; and what is more
*Have you ever been experienced* than
Jimi Hendrix blasting from a passing
predawn car, more requisite
than the ring of fire: that all things
called true must leap through; and what,
if anything, is less peripheral,
the *least* peripheral, more within you
than your path beyond compass?

After Reading the Greatest War Story


I tried to reimagine man's nature.
Working overtime, with my team of wishful
thinkers, we revised what seems simple:
the one thousand ships about to be launched
will not be launched: irresponsible love-stricken
Paris, although scrumptious in his polished
armor of self, will turn responsible—but wait—

over there—beneath that dark foreboding
storm cloud, my team of thinkers are shaking
their heads, drained and complaining: there's no way
around it: irresponsible love-stricken
Paris, in his full armor of obstinacy,
won't be changed. The one thousand ships
about to be launched will be launched.

Briefly the Mourning Cloaks

These butterflies do not soar.
They have no choreographed war dance.
No fleets, no swift movements in practiced formation.
The mourning cloaks have no plan.

Here and there, they appear without context.
They settle on foliage in snatches:
in a garden, in a lone shrub. By the curbside,

one lands on the ragged surface of a Queen Anne's Lace.
Basking in the dangerous heat, its dark
velvet out-stretched wings, a shroud of premonition:
*take notice*: the morning cloaks have no vote.
They have no policies. They have no cash.
Each one, the letter sent.

Like a translator, I've taken liberties:
risking meaning for the iridescent blue dabs
running with a message: *remember, goodbye,*
above the gilded edge of their wings.

Spillage

To distill brevity, poured libation
in the cup of trembling, to drink the hard
rhythmic rain. The wind and black rain hammer
the leaves and mourning cloak. Wings drop
ink-dark perfections, their fragile gold edges
disintegrate into the grass. Beware
of the gilded wings' dust into lyric.
Hear it make rounds through the assembly hall,
hear it ring around a hero's ankle
then settle, sprinkled like a potion,
into the trembling cup that cannot hold.

II

We Can Repair the Canoe

When I found our book, its leaves
were autumnal, red oak and crumbling.
It needed mending, but a song could heal us.

While searching for lyrics, in my mind
I could be with you. Running parallel to that
I'm floating down river:

in one scenario: left alone,
I'm up creek, you know, without the paddle.

In scenario two: waterfalls, white
rapids, the foam-covered rock—split
goes the beautiful birch.

The crack and crunch of it copied
to my brain like a CD. Ripped. Remastered.
Remixed: I hear our river song.

Robert Johnson

met the devil. Some say that's a myth.
Did he go with the flow? Maybe he stumbled
singing his know, *dark gonna catch me here…*

Things happen at midnight: in stories, songs,
retractable fibs—or look at it this way:

things happen in the head. Down river or down
the tracks contradictions spin in my head.

Maybe I'll fall when the train leaves the station.
Maybe I'll scowl when the train's coming in.

Here's what I say when my head feels dead, Don't
stop—words go living in a world called out.

Some say Robert Johnson met the devil.
I can't know, but despite all the mumble,
the voice of trepidation is lone as the owl's.

Let Me Not Reject Catharsis

The sky was cobalt blue, and the stone
chimeras on the corners of the bell tower—
I think I heard their scream.

I wasn't frightened. I heard
the pure unheard, a sustained note
as strange as themselves, as distracting
as a neon's soundless advertisement
red-glowing in its cursive-shaped tube, luring
someone like me, the insatiable.

But I think, from this runic choir
in the cobalt blue sky, what I heard
or felt was sublime emptiness.

In the Key of Night minor

Above the intersection
my window rattles. Here comes night's last bus,
the heavy rolling Ship of Death.

What's left beneath a seat? a book
of Lawrence poems, a pocket atlas
of Man's shame, or a gun.

I think the pavement covers
what long ago were paths to sacred
groves and singing streams.

The bother of boulevards
and streets neither holds its tongue
nor leads us to a hilltop.

I hear clanging, but it's not
too edgy—a tussle? or someone
at the curb with empties.

The crosswalk's digital icon
of the little man is flashing:
*walk across the street with purpose:*

it's time to cross
from this side to the other.

Notes:

"Familial": This poem is dedicated to all families.

"I Will Wait for Eternity": In memory of Katherine Adams.

"Space to Proceed": This poem is dedicated to John Harn.

Thank you, many times over, to my friends Jack Sullivan and Carolyn Berge for their generosity and support while I lived in Ann Arbor from 2019 to 2022 during which most of the poems in this chapbook were written.

Thank you to John Harn for his editorial comments on several poems in this chapbook.

# Something from Nothing

John Peter Harn

And if, after all
the years spent looking,
you find your soul holds nothing more
than what you put there yourself?

I

*- not everything born has been conceived -*

\*

Instead of rain, dust.

An accumulation.

People slipping away.

Debris and the absence of debris.

Headstones back to the quarry, fossils back to dust.

Vertigo and torque.

An endless zooming out.

No topsoil. Basalt.

Dust but no rain.

*

Off I go on foot again
down another trail to the Pleistocene
tracking the trackless old ones.


I know I won't meet
any other hikers here
but I have my walking stick
the Polestar
and, as always
half-a-day out from wherever I am

tumbling meltwater.

*

The first light was amber light.
Other light came from it.


It's what the Call to Prayer
calls to,

what we see behind our children's eyes
and they behind ours,

what we feel when we open
a lover's fingers and touch their palm.


My me, your you,
it floods the room in the blessed last.

\*

When conditions are perfect,

at the point of equinox…
or along the shadow-line of a racing eclipse…
or wherever the Milky Way is
bright enough to throw shadows…

ancient shorelines sometimes glimpse
the arc of their long lineages.


I understood this late last night
lying on my back on my living room floor
chasing the blades of a ceiling fan
through the daydream loophole.

\*

If the earth were an organism
and species were its organs
and humans were a cancer upon it,

why wouldn't the earth
send a heatwave like a fever
to throw us off stride
and a virus like a swarm
of white blood cells to kill us
and polar floods and wildfires
to cleanse and cauterize the wound.

Why wouldn't the earth
heal itself and not look back.

*

On NPR, a man says racoons
are more scientific than we
that they're not lost, like us
in the gap between
what evidence is and isn't.


To make his point, he asks us to imagine
a group of racoons are nearly wiped out
by a flood or wildfire.
Would the survivors insist
on a supernatural cause?


He wants us to emit less heat,
spend time with photosynthesis,
be more attuned
to the hidden lives of bees.

\*

The disease is you at work
   sitting at your computer
   like a pile of sand after the dump truck pulls away.


The cure is standing in your kitchen
   filling a kettle with tap water
   waiting for the whistle.


The recovery is holding a #2 pencil
   writing, *Little black seeds are warming up,*
   crossing it out.

\*

What if people routinely recalled
the moment they were conceived,

if throughout our long history
we'd always remembered
when our sperm found our egg
and the how-and-why we surged into being
was just another thing we knew
like the name of our fourth grade teacher.


What kind of world
would we have today instead,
absent metaphor and art.

*

A hand hovers over a bowl
of every kind and color of fruit.


It chooses something…
puts it back,

chooses something else…
puts it back.

II

*Geography means destiny.*

- Ibn Khaldun -

\*

There was a place
in time once
in what we call the City of New York
where lilacs and strawberries
glazed the back-yard summers
of a little girl and her big sister.

A place in footnotes now
where love washed over
them and their soft parents
and a grandmother needlepointing
down the hall.

Lilacs bloomed, the story goes
either side of the backyard table
where, on Sunday afternoons
strawberries were eaten
al fresco with cream
and the Victrola was set up for opera.

A place that lives
in two dark photos now
tucked inside a book
and this short string of hopeful words
striving against the page.

\*

They discuss the gallery's new exhibit
over onion soup and a crusty baguette
and split the bill in half.

They take their time walking back
to her corner apartment in the old part of town.

Standing under a streetlight
she touches his hand
and invites him up for a glass of wine.

They toss their jackets over a chair.
She uncorks a bottle with a *shhlunk*
and pours two glasses.

He puts *La Vie En Rose*
by Edith Piaf on the turntable.

They listen in silence.
When the music stops
she takes the glass from his hand
and puts it on the table.

She leans in close
warm words in his ear,
> *If not for you, my love,*
> *who would I sail away with?*

Ocean waves in the plush
upholstery of her floral divan.

\*

He's thinking Burma
might be a good place to retire,
Burma being warm and shaped by Buddhists
smiling in the absence of tools.

He can see himself living
on tea and brown rice
useless shoes by the door, in Burma.

Maybe he'd teach English
part time for a perfunctory coin,
befriend a student's grandfather
and treat him to a nostalgic tour
of the threadbare village he grew up in
up north somewhere, in Burma.

He could help a venerable old gentleman like that
find his mother's neglected grave,
sweep it clean as it emerged
from behind an incense curl, in Burma.

They could spend the afternoon tending it
pouring thimbles of strong rice wine,
toasting her and each other
until, bottle-drained and drunk
they fell asleep in the Burmese shade
where Death found them
but passed them by,
pretending to be deceived.

The more he thinks about Burma,
the better it gets.
The more he says it, the more it just clicks.

\*

He endures the Toledo skyline
from the window of a Trailways bus,
the deceptive emptiness of Pennsylvania,
hairpin turns on the road to Manhattan.

In his backpack, the topaz bracelet
he bought for her in Des Moines,
scented stationery, loose rice,
unsent letters tied up in string.

He waits for her at their prearranged place
on a bench in a museum
that holds the extinct rhinoceros,
but she doesn't show.

At closing time, he leaves his pack on the bench
and walks the thirty blocks back to his hotel.

Stanwyck and Cooper on pay-per-view.
Jim Beam and a bucket of ice.
The hulking gleam of the ice machine.

Out on the fire escape at 4 AM.
Blanket and pillow from his room.
Waiting for the sun to launch
another day in this hungry age of science.

\*

Let's say you really are
sprawled out on sheepskin
on a rocky Aegean outcrop
touching a sphere in a daydream…

and let's say those footprints behind you
really are all left feet…

and that rainbow behind you
really does swivel out of view
every time you turn to look.

It means you've been busy
re-glossing the *Principia*, gulping salty air
getting ready to pass
through the Pillars of Hercules.


Still undone is building a sail
from whatever's lying around
to catch Polaris's wind.

\*

In the news today, the James Webb Telescope
found organic molecules in a galaxy
12 billion light years from Earth
proving complex chemistry
started much earlier than we thought.

It's one of the oldest galaxies ever observed
existing 12 billion years ago
and one of the youngest
seen at 10% of its current age.

A miniscule fraction of the galaxy's output
collided with the telescope's collector.
The rest, if it doesn't hit something
will someday catch up with the edge of the Universe
which is expanding more slowly than the speed of light
and can't outrun it.

Reading this article, re-reading it,
is like slowing to a crawl on the interstate
to gawk at an 18-wheeler,
jack-knifed, on its side,
belching flames in the median.

Sometimes we need to see the marrow splayed.
Step backwards off a cliff.

\*

They're lingering over coffee
after breakfast, in a restaurant, somewhere in Japan.
It's 1986. They're thirty-something, American.
Morning sun sidelights their faces.
She takes out her Nikon, snaps a photo of him
and passes the camera over the table.
He takes one of her and passes it back.
No flash. Morning sun sidelights their faces.
When the prints come back from the store
they're wearing the same expression:
eyebrows up, huge pupils
lips parted, about to say something
to the wind.

# III

*- and the weather is sublime -*

\*

*for JB*

Emptyhanded, with a thousand-yard stare
I sit where I used to hold you
in the rocking chair by the window
but you're somewhere else now
grown but not past rocking
sipping coffee maybe
on the fringes of a university
finding patterns in the slowly crashing wave
of an ordinary day.

If you call I'll tell you robins returned
to the nest in our back yard
where years ago I perched you
and your sister on a ladder
to peer in at paper-thin chicks
gaping mouths at us
despite how close we were
or because of it.

You won't remember my arms
binding the three of us together
so we could lean in for a better view
or the speckled-down gullets in the nest
reaching up for us, sensing what we sensed
that we had enough love to feed them too.

But I remember it clearly
that far-off day in a world still young,
and record it here for you.

*for Dotty (1925-2009)*

It mattered, while it lasted
the cluster of people and places you knew
their intersections and alignments
your habits and beliefs, your folkways and ritual.
There was a totality in your trove
an entirety made up
of seeing and being seen
and the needs you found and met
in the hearts you knew by heart.
It was a universe, no less, your history and lore
your encyclopedia of knowing, the layers of care.
But when you passed, it passed too
stretched and segmented, became a lost form.
People who loved you tried but couldn't
keep it braided any more
than a month or two
and even then they only saved
the edge where light sliced the dark.
And before long, even that was lost
racing off as photons will
in every direction
beyond any real retrieval or repair.

\*
*for Nene and Meme*

My two girls
still sleeping side-by-side after eighteen years
beds pushed as close as physics allow
dreaming each other's dream.

Tomorrow you're both off to college again
where you'll dive deep into canvases I won't see
which is, I almost admit, as it should be.

You don't know how many nights
I stood in your doorway when you were small
checking in on you before I slept
standing on the threshold
where your milestones found my love
unwrapped in the dark
and I was reborn in the scent of cut hay.

But I want you to know
thousands of my days closed with that
ritual tenderness for you.

Part of me will only remember you
as you were then
small and sharing a blanket
I was somehow allowed to weave for you.

*That I was gifted daughters
who dream sister dreams…*

\*

*for my newborn granddaughter,*
*across an ocean, on another continent*

Months from now
when you're taken to the beach for the first time
and held above the waves
and slowly lowered
feet first in the foam,
if you kick and cry from being
so close to the abyss,
someone who loves you will lift you up
and hold you against their chest
and you'll bury your face in that familiar calm,
      but that person won't be me.

And when you're sick some year
as you surely will be
with one of the deadly childhood diseases
lost in fever and blinded by tears,
someone who loves you will fight for your life
siphon your pain
and carry you safely to the other side,
      and that person too, won't be me.

But for one week, Sara
when you were newborn
I got to hold you against the chill,
see myself in your eyes
and plant sweet nicknames in the folds of your warm neck.

\*

We were alive
it was postwar, and my brother and I
six and four, were given grownup shovels
and permission to dig
all the way to China
to settle whether it was possible.
This was a huge improvement
over parenting in the 30s
when our parents grew up
and digging was understood
to be *verboten*.
So kudos to them for helping us see
there were ways to find things out.
Steps one could take.
And kudos to them for giving us maps
of Ike's expanding motorways
when we turned eighteen, and wheels to find
the Oregon Trail for ourselves.
And when I say *we* I mean
Danny and me. And when I say *postwar* I mean
when is it ever not? And when I say *dig*
I mean we knew full well we were testing a theory.
And when I say *parents*, I mean those two souls
who won the war and had the guts
to populate the peace with the likes of us
to give us lives we couldn't request
but would've, had we known.

\*

In Eugene Oregon, people cared enough
to dedicate a park bench to Pac-Man
a homeless man beaten to death
by drunken fools he didn't know.

At the sentencing, the judge told the murderers,
  *Mr. Bishop was a human being. He had worth.*
  *People cared about him. He had friends.*
  *He was a welcome member of this community.*
  *You are not.*

Someone filled out the forms, gathered donations
wrote the inscription for the brass plaque:
  *In memory of Pac-Man*
  *and our other homeless friends who died too soon,*
and the bench was installed in Skinner Butte Park
not far from the scene of the crime.

People cared enough
to plant a backstop against apathy,
to face forward when they could've looked aside.


Fifteen years after, I'm sitting on Pac-Man's bench
within earshot of the Willamette River.
It's a Monday in late June.
Children play on a climbing structure
people are walking, riding bikes
and the weather is sublime.

\*

It's Memorial Day
at Luper Pioneer Cemetery, outside Eugene.

Fifty people gather to pay respects
to stones from the 1850s.

Half the stones are illegible.
All have lost weight.

Descendants are here, and armchair historians
everyone righteous
with second-hand knowledge of unknowable things.

I say hello to an old vet in a beret
shading his eyes, leaning on a cane
looking up at giant oaks'
empathetic branches.

He sizes me up.
*These trees have ancestors too,* he finally says.

To anyone else, I might've answered:
  *Later, after we all go home*
  *these trees will dapple moonlight*
  *on these disappearing stones*
  *while we toss in our soft beds*
  *dreaming of our possessions…*

but can't muster my trademark
pretense in his presence,
shading my eyes instead,
looking up like him.

\*

They took down the tallest tree
on my street today. Killed it
though we didn't think of it that way
at first. Neighbors gathered
to chat above the chipper
watch hard hats and gloves cut limbs into decades
lower them with ropes and
deconstruct them on the ground.
Width first. Then height.
Use its weight against it.
We couldn't see if there was reverence
in the workers' faces, so intent they were
on cutting. We wondered if the tree had rot
or aggressive roots, or obstructed a driveway pour
why it found the end of its tenure today
when its rings, even at the base, were still clear.
A neighbor said the tree had lived
because people planted it
a century ago for shade
but no one cared for parsing anymore
now that the deed was done.
The crew, spent, loaded the debris
into battered trucks and drove away
while the neighbors, forgetting how they came
staggered off in ones and twos
drunk on sap and butchered wood
searching the ground for souvenirs.

*

A lot of what I feel here
at the end of my seventh decade
reminds me of that old sofa we had
out on the porch those years
we lived on Grand River Avenue.

The bell-bottom years.
And the sunshine that illuminated them
and those lavish good times we spent
under the influence of stars.

Today I'm wondering what if
we gave the working poor
sofas like that, to soften the pressure
points of injustice.

And if we gave every parent
who ever lost a child, born or unborn
sofas like that, places to float
in the dreamscape of the forgiven.

Just a simple, old sofa.
Rib-worn, a little too soft
out of the rain on a covered wooden porch
available to anyone
belonging to no one
some small comfort on the side of the road.

\*

We're chatting
under the influence,
slouched in comfortable chairs.


You ask me if I think
the rhythm in us
is in everything else,
animate and inanimate,
if we might not have
any special claim.


*That could well be...* I say
and ask, if so,
if you think it all traces back
to some common spring
and endlessly manifests
scaled up and scaled down.


*Probably...* you say,
*since it's in touch.*

Notes

Pg 60.  *If the earth were an organism*
is for Carol Durak, whose reaction to it in an earlier form caused me to pull it from the scrap pile.

Pg 66.  *There was a place*  and  Pg 75.  *It mattered, while it lasted*
are for my mother, Dorothy Jean Fusaro Harn.

Pg 72.  *They're lingering over coffee*
The woman in the poem is the photographer Jeanne Maasch.

Pg 74.  *Emptyhanded, with a thousand yard stare*
is for my middle daughter, Jessica Aya.

Pg 76.  *My two girls*
is for my two youngest daughters, Jessica Aya and Michelle Megumi.

Pg 77.  *Months from now*
is for my granddaughter, Sara, who lives in England.

Pg 78.  *We were alive*
is for my parents, Paul H Harn Jr. (1921-1974) and Dorothy J Fusaro (1925-2009).

Pg 81.  *They took down the tallest tree*
is dedicated to the poet Stephanie Pilar, who, commenting on her love for nature, says, *Every tree belongs to me!*

Pg 82.  *A lot of what I feel here*
was written with my friend Michael Warholak in mind, whom I shared a house with in East Lansing, Michigan in the mid-1970s.

About the Authors

**RODGER MOODY** is the founding editor of Silverfish Review Press. His poems have appeared in many magazines, including *Caliban, Mudfish,* and *ZYZZYVA*. He has been the recipient of the C. Hamilton Baily Fellowship in Poetry from Literary Arts in Portland, Oregon and was twice awarded a residential fellowship in poetry from the Fine Arts Work Center in Provincetown. *History*, a full-length collection of poetry was published in 2015 by sight | for | sight books.

**CAROL DURAK** lived in various parts of the country before settling in Maine, where, in addition to writing, she made a living in book restoration and conservation. Leaving the East Coast in 2019, she spent three years in Ann Arbor, Michigan, where most of the poems in this chapbook were written. Her poems have appeared in *Antioch Review, Cimarron Review, Laurel Review, New Letters, Shenandoah,* and other journals. She lives in New Mexico.

**JOHN HARN** grew up outside Detroit. In high school, he learned from Richard Brautigan that poems can be about anything. John has published three poetry collections, *Physics for Beginners* (Blue Light Book Award), *Witness* (Aldrich) and *Mostly the Wind* (Flowstone). He recently exhibited poems with photographer Jeanne Maasch at several Oregon art galleries and self-published, through a grant from Lane Arts Council, a book combining Oregon history with original poetry. A father of 3 and a grandfather of 2 ½, he lives in Eugene.

About the Artist

**SIENA SANDERSON** studied painting and music at the University of Oregon, overlapping the time when Rodger, Carol, and John studied poetry there. She lives in Arroyo Seco, New Mexico where she works in the community supporting families and young children and continues to draw in her studio at the base of the Sangre de Christo mountains.

About the Typeface

The interior text is set in Adobe Minion Pro, a serif typeface designed by Robert Slimbach and released in the early 1990s. It was inspired by typefaces created in the late Renaissance era, an innovative period that produced elegant and highly readable type designs. Although Minion has a baroque form, it works well in modern applications. The name comes from the traditional naming system for type sizes, in which *Minion* is between *Nonpareil* and *Brevier*. Minion was designed for body text in a classic style, although it is slightly condensed with larger apertures to increase legibility. According to designer Robert Slimbach, the Minion typeface has *"a simplified structure and moderate proportions."*

www.ingramcontent.com/pod-product-compliance
Lightning Source LLC
Chambersburg PA
CBHW030345100526
44592CB00010B/831